First World War
and Army of Occupation
War Diary
France, Belgium and Germany

30 DIVISION
90 Infantry Brigade
London Regiment
2/14 Battalion (London Scottish)
1 June 1918 - 31 August 1919

WO95/2340/2

The Naval & Military Press Ltd
www.nmarchive.com
Published in association with The National Archives

Published by

The Naval & Military Press Ltd

Unit 10 Ridgewood Industrial Park,

Uckfield, East Sussex,

TN22 5QE England

Tel: +44 (0) 1825 749494

www.naval-military-press.com

www.nmarchive.com

This diary has been reprinted in facsimile from the original. Any imperfections are inevitably reproduced and the quality may fall short of modern type and cartographic standards.

© **Crown Copyright**
Images reproduced by permission of The National Archives, London, England, 2015.

Contents

Document type	Place/Title	Date From	Date To
Heading	30th Division 90th Infy Bde 2-14th London Regt. (London Scottish) Jun 1918-Aug 1919 From Egypt To Div 179 Bde		
Heading	War Diary of the 2/14th Bn. London Regiment. (London Scottish) for the month of June, 1918. Volume No IV		
War Diary	In The Field	01/06/1918	30/06/1918
Heading	2/14. Bn. London Regiment. (London Scottish.) War Diary From 1st. July to 31st. July. 1918. Vol 2		
War Diary	Serques. Pas de Calais	01/07/1918	07/07/1918
War Diary	Ebblinghem	08/07/1918	08/07/1918
War Diary	Eecke	09/07/1918	27/07/1918
War Diary	In The Field	28/07/1918	31/07/1918
Heading	War Diary 2/14th. Bn. London Regiment (London Scottish) for month of August 1918 Vol 3		
War Diary	In The Field	01/08/1918	31/08/1918
Miscellaneous	Appendix 1. Casualties.		
Miscellaneous	Appendix I. Account of Operation taking place between night 20/21st Aug and 23/24th Aug 1918	23/08/1918	23/08/1918
Heading	War Diary 2/14 Bn London Regt (London Scottish) September 1918 Vol 4		
War Diary	In The Field	01/09/1918	30/09/1918
Miscellaneous	Appendix I. 2/14th Bn. London Regt (London Scottish) account of Operations of 2nd/3rd. Sept 1918.	02/09/1918	02/09/1918
Heading	2/4th London Regt. October 1918		
Heading	War Diary Of The 2/14. London (Scottish) Regiment For The Month Of October 1918 (Volume 28)		
War Diary	In The Field	01/10/1918	31/10/1918
Miscellaneous	Appendix I Operations 14th-21st October.	14/10/1918	14/10/1918
Heading	War Diary of the 2/14th. Bn. London Regiment (London Scottish) for the month of November 1918. Vol 6		
War Diary	In The Field.	01/11/1918	30/11/1918
Heading	2/14th. Bn. London Regiment. (London Scottish) War Diary for the month of December 1918. Vol 7		
War Diary	In The Field	01/12/1918	04/12/1918
War Diary	Les Ciseaux	05/12/1918	09/12/1918
War Diary	Les Ciseaux and La Lacque	10/12/1918	23/12/1918
War Diary	La Lacque	24/12/1918	31/12/1918
Heading	War Diary For the month of January 1919. 2/14th. Bn. London Regiment (London Scottish) Vol 8		
War Diary	La Lacque	01/01/1919	02/01/1919
War Diary	In The Field	03/01/1919	06/01/1919
War Diary	Etaples	07/01/1919	31/01/1919
Heading	2/14th. Bn. London Regiment. (London Scottish). War Diary. For Month Ending. February 1919. Vol 9		
War Diary	Etaples.	01/02/1919	06/02/1919
War Diary	Le Gouffre	07/02/1919	28/02/1919
Heading	War Diary Of The 2/14. London Regiment For The Month Of March 1919 Vol 10		

War Diary	Le Gouffre (Le Touquet)	01/03/1919	28/03/1919
War Diary	Etaples	29/03/1919	31/03/1919
Heading	War Diary Of The 2/14th Battalion London Regiment For The Month Of April 1919 Vol 11		
War Diary	Etaples	01/04/1919	30/04/1919
Heading	War Diary Of The 2/14th Battalion London Regiment For The Month Of May 1919 Vol 12		
War Diary	Etaples	01/05/1919	24/05/1919
War Diary	Abbeville	25/05/1919	31/05/1919
Heading	War Diary Of 2/14th Battalion. London Regiment. (London Scottish) For Month Of June 1919. Vol 13		
Miscellaneous	D.D. 18/6	01/07/1919	01/07/1919
War Diary	Abbeville	01/06/1919	30/06/1919
Heading	2/14th Battalion London Regiment. (London Scottish) War Diary For Month Of July 1919. Vol 14		
War Diary	Abbeville	01/07/1919	31/07/1919
Heading	War Diary of 2/14th Battalion London Regiment. (London Scottish). for Month Of August 1919.		
War Diary	Abbeville	01/08/1919	31/08/1919

30TH DIVISION
90TH INFY BDE

2-14TH LONDON REGT.
(LONDON SCOTTISH)
JUN 1918-AUG 1919

FROM EGYPT
60 DIV 179 BDE

(6339) Wt. W160/M3016 1,500,000 10/17 McA & W Ltd (E 1898) Forms W3091.   Army Form W.3091.

Cover for Documents.

Nature of Enclosures.

CONFIDENTIAL.

VOLUME No. IV

W A R   D I A R Y

----of the------

2/14th Bn. LONDON REGIMENT,
(LONDON SCOTTISH)

for the month of J U N E , 1 9 1 8.

....................Lt.Col.,
Commanding 2/14th Bn. LONDON REGIMENT,
(London Scottish).

IN THE FIELD.

4th July, 1918.

Notes, or Letters written.

Army Form C. 2118.

WAR DIARY of 2/14 Bn London Regiment INTELLIGENCE SUMMARY.

(Erase heading not required.)

Place	Date	Hour	Summary of Events and Information	Remarks and references to Appendices
In the Field	June 1		The Battalion entrained at FUZA for KANTARA.	MR
	2		The Battalion arrived at KANTARA.	MR
	3		Company training under Company Commanders. Specialist classes:- Signalling, Scouts and Snipers, Lewis gun + R.S.M's class. Bathing in Canal.	MR
	4		Training under Coy Commanders. Gas Course for N.C.O's	MR
	5		Divine Service	MR
	6		Training as 3rd inst. Gas class contd. Bathing	MR
	7-14		Training as yesterday	RM
	15		Coy & Specialist Training. Bathing + washing. Gas Training. Bn entrained KANTARA 1700 hours. Left KANTARA 1840 hours	RM
	16		Arrived ALEXANDRIA 0315 hours. Embarked on H.M.T. CANBERRA 0800 hours	RM
	17		Remained on board H.M.T. CANBERRA. Physical drill, Lewis gun and Musketry Training carried out	RM
	18		Left ALEXANDRIA 1700 hours.	RM
	19-21		Bn. arrived TARANTO 1200 hours (21st inst) at 1800 hours proceeded into inner harbour. Remained on board during night. 21 - 22.	RM
	22		Bn disembarked and proceeded to CIMINO Rest Camp TARANTO.	RM

Army Form C. 2118.

WAR DIARY
or
INTELLIGENCE SUMMARY.
(Erase heading not required.)

Place	Date	Hour	Summary of Events and Information	Remarks and references to Appendices
[the Field]	23		Physical training and Bathing	
	24		Entrained at CIMINO Station leaving there at 0523 hours. Passed through BRINDISI & BARI.	
	25		FOGGIA. TERMOLI, CASTELAMARE. ADRIATICO. ANCONA.	
	26		FAENZA BOLOGNA, PIACENZA VOGHERA	
	27		SAMPIERDARENA. SAVONA. VENTIMIGLIA, CANNES LA BOCCA	
	28		MARSEILLES. MIRAMAS AVIGNON. LE TEIL.	
	29		ST. GERMAIN AU MONT D'OR. PARAY LE MONIAL MALASHERBES	
	30		US. MARINES. SERQUEUX NOYELLE.	

Army Form W.3091.

Cover for Documents.

CONFIDENTIAL

Nature of Enclosures.

2/14th. Bn. London Regiment. (London Scottish.)

WAR DIARY

From 1st. JULY to 31st. JULY. 1918.

2/8/18.

J. Edgar
for Major.
Comdg. 2/14th. Bn. London Regiment.
(London Scottish)

Notes, or Letters written.

Army Form C. 2118.

WAR DIARY
or
INTELLIGENCE SUMMARY.
(Erase heading not required.)

Instructions regarding War Diaries and Intelligence Summaries are contained in F.S. Regs., Part II. and the Staff Manual respectively. Title pages will be prepared in manuscript.

Place	Date 1918	Hour	Summary of Events and Information	Remarks and references to Appendices
SERQUES. Pas de Calais	July	1.	Battalion detrained at AUDRUICQ and proceeded to billeting area SERQUES. Sheet 27 a S.E. R.7.a.6.4.	HAZEBROUCK Sheet 27
"	"	2	Companies were at disposal of O.C. Coys. Kit inspection was carried out. A party of officers & NCOs attended one day Gas Course under Bran. Gas officer.	
"	"	3.	Specialist training in Lewis Gun, musketry, Signalling classes. Training for companies and tactical scheme for Officers carried out on Battalion training ground during morning.	
"	"	4	Specialist training as usual. Training for commanders and tactical scheme for company commanders on same area.	
"	"	5.	Specialist training in afternoon only except for Signallers Stretcher bearers. Battalion Field Day on usual area.	
"	"	6.	Specialist training as yesterday with exception of musketry Classes. Battalion Field Day on usual area.	
"	"	7	Church parade in morning. Advance party went forward to RENINSCOUR.	
"	"	8	Battalion moved KEBBLINGHEM	
EBBLINGHEM	"	9	Battalion moved to EECKE becoming Corps Reserve.	
EECKE	"	10	Specialist training. Company, Platoon, Section Commanders reconnoitred the BERTHEN line of defence.	
"	"	11	Specialist training in morning, on night 11/12 battalion marched taking up position at Mt DES CATS in the BERTHEN line.	
"	"	12	Specialist training in afternoon. Coys at disposal of O.C. Coys.	
"	"	13	Inspection in morning by Army Commander at SYLVESTRE CAPPEL.	
"	"	14	Church parade in morning	

WAR DIARY
or
INTELLIGENCE SUMMARY.
(Erase heading not required.)

Army Form C. 2118.

Place	Date	Hour	Summary of Events and Information	Remarks and references to Appendices
ECKE	July	15	Specialist training all day. Companies in new training area.	Sheet 27 1/40000
"	"	16	Gas training all day.	
"	"	17	Specialist training in morning. Moved up to MT KOKEREELE R16d. & R17c. night 17/18 July. Trekking having new battle stations.	
"	"	18	Battalion arrived back in billets 8 a.m. 'C' Coy relieved 'D' Coy on MT des CATS in evening. Specialist & Company training in afternoon.	
"	"	19	Usual training.	
"	"	20	Bayonet fighting + Kit Inspection. The Commanding Officer inspected billets and company lines.	
"	"	21	Church parades in morning.	
"	"	22	Gas Demonstration in morning. Companies carried out digging practice and Specialist as usual in afternoon. 'B' Coy relieved 'C' Coy on MT des CATS.	
"	"	23	Rain prevented aeroplane demonstration in morning. Specialists in afternoon.	
"	"	24	Witnessed demonstration of "Co-operation of Aircraft and Infantry." Specialist training in afternoon.	
"	"	25	Specialist training and Bayonet fighting all day.	
"	"	26	Morning - Training suspended owing to rain. Specialist training in afternoon.	
"	"	27	1 Battalion relieved 18th (G.I.) H.L.I. in reserve positions at R8c95. (Mole Farm)	BERTHEN

Army Form C. 2118.

WAR DIARY
or
INTELLIGENCE SUMMARY.
(Erase heading not required.)

Instructions regarding War Diaries and Intelligence Summaries are contained in F. S. Regs., Part II. and the Staff Manual respectively. Title pages will be prepared in manuscript.

Place	Date	Hour	Summary of Events and Information	Remarks and references to Appendices
In the field	28/7/18	—	Battalion remained in Brigade Reserve at R.8.c.8.6	1/M BERTHEN + METEREN 1/20000
	29/7/18		Advance parties proceeded to take preliminary to taking over the front line from 2/15 LONDON REGT. BN. HQ. of 2/15th BN. at M.27.b.8.b	1/M LOCRE 1/10000
	30/7/18		Proceeded from Reserve to relieve 2/15 London Regt. in the line, with Headquarters M.27.b.8.6	
	31/7/18		Relieved the 2/15 London. Dispositions of Companies in the line distributed on Left "A" Right, "C" Right Centre, "B" Left Centre, "D" Left (Assembly) 3 O.R.'s killed and 3 wounded	
	31/7/18		Effective Strength — 927 all ranks. Capt. L.W. Noble. 14th Londons joined Bn. from 25th July 2/Lts. R.D. Cotton. " " " 26th " " K.W. Gauld. " " " 26th " " C. Gregory. " " " 28" " " J.Y. Dimbleby. " " " 29" "	

(6392) Wt. W6192/P875 1,500,000 4/18 McA & W Ltd (E 2815) Forms W3091/4.   Army Form W.3091.

Cover for Documents.

Nature of Enclosures.

CONFIDENTIAL

WAR DIARY

2/14th. Bn. London Regiment (London Scottish)

for month of

AUGUST 1918

for Major.
Comdg. 2/14th Bn. London Regiment
(London Scottish)

2/9/18

Notes, or Letters written.

2/14 Bn. London Regt.
(London Scottish)

Army Form C. 2118.

WAR DIARY
or
INTELLIGENCE SUMMARY.
(Erase heading not required.)

Instructions regarding War Diaries and Intelligence Summaries are contained in F.S. Regs., Part II. and the Staff Manual respectively. Title pages will be prepared in manuscript.

Place	Date	Hour	Summary of Events and Information	Remarks and references to Appendices
In the Field	1/8/18		Bn. in the line, with H.Q. at LOCRE Sector. Right Sub sector "B" Coy on Right "C" Coy Right Centre "A" Coy in the line with H.Q at M.27. & 7.3. "D" Coy left Centre and "D" Coy left of Coy. Casualties from enemy shelling and M.G fire 5 killed and 9 wounded.	LOCRE 1/1000–0
			Bn. was relieved by 2/16 th 4Bn. London Regt (Queens Westminsters) and proceeded in Reserve Area with H.Q at R 2 d 1.0.	BERTHEN 1/1000–0 LOCRE 1/1000–0
	2/8/18		In billets and bivouacs in Reserve Area. At dusk moved up to take support from to Right Sub sector LOCRE Sector with H.Q at M 21 C 5 4.	SHEET BERTHEN 1/10000
	3/8/18		Bn proceeded to Bivouac Area at EECKE.	Sheet
	4/8/18		Church parade in morning.	
	5/8/18		Companies under Coy. Commanders for training in morning. Specialists for training in afternoon.	
	6/8/18		– do –	
	7/8/18		Companies under Coy. Commanders in morning. E.O. (Major White) inspected A and C Coys in full marching order, and Band in Fighting order in afternoon.	
	8/8/18		Bn under Coy. Comdrs in morning. Bn arrived in evening left Bn to entrain at Rgn 4.5.1. Plus 275 Station History B. Section electric light at NEZ Receipt A.3 Camp at ARMEKE	NEZEKEM

Army Form C. 2118.

WAR DIARY
or
INTELLIGENCE SUMMARY.

(Erase heading not required.)

2/5th Bn London R of R
(London Scottish)

Instructions regarding War Diaries and Intelligence Summaries are contained in F. S. Regs., Part II. and the Staff Manual respectively. Title pages will be prepared in manuscript.

Place	Date	Hour	Summary of Events and Information	Remarks and references to Appendices
In the field	9/8/18		Training under Company Commanders and specialist training including Lewis gun, signalling, Scouts, Stretcher Bearers, Range finders, Lasers.	Sgd
				Sgd
	10/8/18		ditto	Sgd
	11/8/18		ditto	Sgd
	12/8/18	9 am	Bathing was in progress during morning until 12.30. During afternoon L.G firing was carried out. Ranges were clean & SB's clean ranged during afternoon. Signalling Class under Sergt Traves from 8-11 am & 2-4 pm	Sgd
	13/8/18	9-11	Coys under Company Commanders for interior economy. Digging tracks in, around Signallers S.B's & Lewis Gun classes as yesterday.	Sgd
		2-4		
	14/8/18	9-11	Coys under Coy Commanders were for interior economy. Digging & practice in attack. Battalion moved to relieve 1/16 Cheshires in the LOCKROP SECTOR. M.2 & 1.5 & 15 M. 29 & 11 em SHEET 28	Sgd 1/20000
	15.8.18		Bn in FRONT LINE.	
	16.8.18		Battn FRONT LINE. During night Battn were relieved in the line by 2/15 Ln R Regiment & moved into SUPPORT took HQ at M 2 a 4.5.	
	17.8.18		Battalion was relieved in SUPPORT line by 2/16th Lond R and moved back into Brigade Reserve at MOTH FARM. (R & C. 90.66).	BERTHEN 1/10000 Ed 15
	18.8.18		Battalion harassed attack twice during day and once by night.	
	19.8.18		Coys under Coy Commanders for interior digging and wiring. Battalion moved up into SUPPORT behind MONT ROUGE (M 22 a) at 9 pm relieving 2/15th Lond R Casualties from shelling 1 Killed O.R, 2 wounded.	KEMMEL St 28 SW 1 1:10000
	20.8.18		Coys moved into assembly positions for attack about 10 pm taking over front line from 2/16 Lond. (See Appendix I.)	

2/14th Bn London Regt
(London Scottish)

Army Form C. 2118.

WAR DIARY
or
INTELLIGENCE SUMMARY.
(Erase heading not required.)

Instructions regarding War Diaries and Intelligence Summaries are contained in F. S. Regs., Part II. and the Staff Manual respectively. Title pages will be prepared in manuscript.

Place	Date	Hour	Summary of Events and Information	Remarks and references to Appendices
In the field	21/8/18		See Appendix I.	
	22/8/18		— do —	
	23/8/18		— do — Battalion moved into SUPPORT behind MONT ROUGE except D Coy which took up position in BLUE LINE in forward slopes of MONT ROUGE. Several casualties from shell fire during relief.	LOOSE 4/rooo w
	24/8/18		Relieved by 2/16 Lond R at 11pm. Moved back to MOTH FARM area into Brigade Reserve. OK	Shut 17 S F 12 rooo w
	25/8/18		No training. C of E church parade	OK
	26/8/18		Kit inspection. No training	OK
	27/8/18		Coys at disposal of OC Coys till 12 noon. Demonstration for Officers signallers on Message Carrying Rockets.	OK
	28/8/18		Coys at disposal of OC Coys until 12 noon. Battn moved up in evening into Cdt SUPPORT behind MONT ROUGE relieving 2/15th Lond R.	LOOSE 4/rooo w
	29/8/18		Specialist training in Signalling Stretcher Bearing.	OK
	30/8/18		Specialist training as yesterday. Battn was due to relieve 2/16th Lond R in FRONT LINE to night, but Germans evacuated their positions and 2/16 R patrols followed up. Battn stood to at half an hour's notice for	

2/14th Bn. London Regt
(London Scottish)

WAR DIARY
or
INTELLIGENCE SUMMARY.

Army Form C. 2118.

Place	Date	Hour	Summary of Events and Information	Remarks and references to Appendices
In the field	30/8/18		an hour or two but 2/16th were relieved by another Bgde from Boyde became reserve.	LUERE 11.00-00 a.a
	31/8/18		Large burial salvage, & working parties at work on DRANOUTRE ridge all day & night.	w.t
			[signature] Major Comdg 2/14 Lond R London Scottish	

APPENDIX 1.

Casualties.

	Officers	Other Ranks
KILLED	2	27

2/Lt. D.C.DUNCAN
2/Lt. H.W.FULLER

WOUNDED	4	89

Lieut. P.H.HOLME
2/Lt. C.GREGORY
2/Lt. R.M.TRIBE
2/Lt. K.W.GAULD

" (GASSED)	1	18

2/Lt. A.N.YOUNG

MISSING	-	5
WOUNDED AT DUTY		13
ACCIDENTALLY INJURED	1	3

2/Lt. J.A.SMITH.

PRISONERS TAKEN

2 Officers and 70 Other ranks.

WAR MATERIAL CAPTURED

5 Heavy Machine Guns

13 Light Machine Guns

2/14 Bn Lond R.
(London Scottish).

(1)

APPENDIX I.

Account of operations taking place between night 20/21st Aug. and 23/24th Aug. 1918.

OBJECTIVE.
Sheet 28. S.W.1.
KEMMEL
1:10000

To capture the DRANOUTRE ridge line. Objective to be from right to left M 35 b 1.6. — M 29. d. 00. 48. — M. 29. d. 40. 32. along line of pond & long ditch to road at M 29 d 17.88.

POSITION of ASSEMBLY.
Sheet — do —

Line of front line from M. 28. d 53. 42. — mound at M 29. a 10. 35. Coys disposed from right to left A, B, & C + 2 platoons D. Remaining 2 Platoons of D Coy in support trenches at M. 29. a. 80 50. The three Coys attacking held approximately 200 yds each.

NARRATIVE.
Sheet — do —

Battalion moved from support line to position of assembly on night 20/21st Aug. 1918. & were all in position by 12.40 midnight. The barrage fell at Zero 2.5 a.m. and the battalion advanced under this heavy barrage and cover of a thick mist. WAKEFIELD WOOD proved a considerable obstacle but was overcome owing to excellence & pace of the artillery barrage. It, however, caused the formations to break up, but section leaders were able to reform on the far side of the wood. All objectives were gained by 3 a.m. Consolidation was commenced but owing to the fact that the right flank was in the air, it was pulled back to conform with the S. Lanc Regt on the right. The Pioneers 6th S.W.B. aided materially in the work of consolidation. Wire was erected in front of support line, also in front of Right Coys front line, but owing to lack time it was not formidable.

APPENDIX. I

Just before the mist lifted, the enemy pressed forward from the direction of DRANOUTRE, and advanced to counter attack. A Coy's covering party were ordered to withdraw at apparently the same time as the counter attack took place, but this was not known when they were ordered to withdraw, and the Lewis Gunner remaining to cover the withdrawal was killed. At the same time the enemy made a formidable counter attack from RUMBOLD FARM to LOCREHOF FARM. The withdrawal of A Coy's Covering party left the Right flank of B Coy in the air and enfiladed by the enemy's attack they together with our Left Post fell back fighting on LOCREHOF FARM, but owing to mist & the unrecognisable condition of the farm itself, fell back past the farm to about M.29.d.00.55. on the corner of the long strip of water in M.29.d.30.50 The enemy rushed in considerable force LOCREHOF FARM causing the Right Post of C Coy to withdraw from the Southern Edge of LOCREHOF POND, establishing himself with a considerable number of Machine Guns in the farm which was then in the air; at the same time attacking along the hedges in M.29.d.80.80. They succeeded in killing or wounding the post & seizing the Lewis Gun. O.C. 'C' Coy Lieut S.E. JONES immediately counter attacked & cleared the Farm, capturing 5 Machine Guns & reached his original right Post again arriving there with a Sergeant & three men. They came under heavy Machine Gun fire from about M.29.d.80.50 and had to withdraw taking with them their Lewis Gun. The post, however, about M.29.d.45.45. was maintained all day under Corpl. DAVIS who was subsequently wounded.

APPENDIX. I.

Broad daylight came suddenly, the mist clearing away; the whole area being under direct observation from KEMMEL thus making movement impossible. During the day 21st Aug. enemy shelling on our line was intermittent. From 10.15 p.m. night 21/22nd the enemy shelled the whole area heavily using a large proportion of gas shells (BLUE & GREEN CROSS) particularly WAKEFIELD WOOD which affected carrying parties. At about midnight the enemy attacked A Coy and the S. LANCS on the right. Right Post of A Coy in conjunction with Left Post S. LANCS repulsed the attack. Enemy succeeded in bombing out next two Posts S. LANCS and established a machine gun at the corner of the fence at about M.35.b.05.70. A Coy threw back a defensive flank & again got touch with S. LANCS but owing to the machine gun and its supporting troops was unable to aid in ejecting the enemy occupying these posts. On the Left flank whilst this was going on 'C' Coy reached a hostile machine gun which had established itself at M.29.d.02.50 killing some of the crew including an officer, but the gun itself was not taken. During 22nd shelling in support line was fairly heavy. On the night 22/23rd 'C' Coy sent out a patrol of 1 officer & 20 men to re-establish themselves in the Post line E of LOCREHOF FARM. but no sooner was the necessary reconnaissance made than the enemy put down a smoke & gas shell bombardment, under cover of which the enemy re-occupied the farm. During the evening two Lewis posts were pushed out to about M.29.d.01.30 and M.29.c.99.05. In the early hours of the morning the battalion was relieved by 2/15th Lond R. and moved back into support behind MONT ROUGE.

Army Form W.3091.

Cover for Documents.

Nature of Enclosures.

Confidential.
War Diary.
2/14 Bn London Regt.
(London Scottish)
September 1918

1/10/18

Comdg 2/14 London Regt
London Scottish

Lt Col.

Notes, or Letters written.

2/14th Bn. London Regt. (London Scottish).   (1.)

Army Form C. 2118.

WAR DIARY
INTELLIGENCE SUMMARY.
(Erase heading not required.)

Place	Date	Hour	Summary of Events and Information	Remarks and references to Appendices
In the field	1/9/18		Still in Bgde. Reserve behind MONT ROUGE. Specialist training as usual.	A/L. Sheet 28. S.W.
— do —	2/9/18		Orders to move up to gds. line in morning.	— do —
— do —	3/9/18		See Appendix I.	— do —
— do —	4/9/18		Became Battalion in Reserve in DONEGAL FARM area N.31.a.9.7.	— do —
— do —	5/9/18		Moved up in/to Support in DAYLIGHT CORNER area N.33.a & c. with BHQ. at N.33.a.3.28. relieving 2/16th Lond R.	— do —
— do —	6/9/18		Still in support. Battalion engaged in carriage work all day	— do —
— do —	7/9/18		— do —	— do —
— do —	8/9/18		Relieved by 7/8th Innishkillings 89th Bgde. Moved back via DRANOUTRE to STARLING F.m M.24.b.20.90. Casualties from shelling during day 2 O.R. wounded	— do —
— do —	9/9/18		Lewis Gun & Sketches Reaver Classes in morning. Moved back to MONT NOIR. M.20.d with BHQ. M.20.d.40.68. Bgde. now in Reserve.	— do —
— do —	10/9/18		Kit Inspection was carried out during morning. Weather bad, rained heavily all day	— do —
— do —	11/9/18		Weather bad in morning Company training & specialist training — L.G., Sketches, Lewis & Scouts — during afternoon	— do —

Lt/Col Comdg 2/14th Bn L.R.
London Scottish

2/14th Bn. London Regt
(London Scottish)

Army Form C. 2118.

WAR DIARY
INTELLIGENCE SUMMARY
(Erase heading not required.)

Instructions regarding War Diaries and Intelligence Summaries are contained in F. S. Regs., Part II. and the Staff Manual respectively. Title pages will be prepared in manuscript.

Place	Date	Hour	Summary of Events and Information	Remarks and references to Appendices
In the field	12/9/18		Divine Service during morning. Co. Commanders presented medal ribbons for DRANOUTRE Ridge & WULVERGHEM actions during afternoon.	
— do —	13/9/18		'C' Coy carried out a tactical scheme during the morning a skeleton force from 'A' & 'B' Coys acting as enemy. L.T.M.B. Detachment co-operated with 'C' Coy giving a demonstration. 'A', 'B' & 'D' Coys supplied R.E. working parties all day as	
— do —	14/9/18		'B' & 'A' Coys carried out tactical schemes on same lines as 'C' Coy. HQ & C Coys	
— do —	15/9/18		Battalion moved to ULSTER CAMP M.35.c.70.05. 'B' Coy to KOUDEKOT CAMP M.34.d.65.20. Sheet 28 SW 'A' & 'D' Coys to LOCRE CHAU CAMP M.34.b.20.90. Bgde became SUPPORT Bgde but retained his billeting demands in camp area. Parties were attached to Line Bgade (2/13) for tactical purposes & in event of necessity were to man the LINDENHOEK – NEUVE EGLISE line. a machine gunners of 1 section per Coy was sent to seventy this line	
— do —	16/9/18		Companies at disposal of O.C. Coys + L.G. training	do —
— do —	17/9/18		Training carried out during day included Lewis Gun training + musketry	do —
— do —	18/9/18		Training as yesterday.	do —
— do —	19/9/18		Battalion relieved from support area to Front Line E of HILL 63 one platoon 2/14 Bn R London Scottish	do —

(2)

Army Form C. 2118.

WAR DIARY
~~INTELLIGENCE SUMMARY~~
(Erase heading not required.)

2/14th Bn London Regt
(Undated)

Instructions regarding War Diaries and Intelligence Summaries are contained in F. S. Regs., Part II. and the Staff Manual respectively. Title pages will be prepared in manuscript.

Place	Date	Hour	Summary of Events and Information	Remarks and references to Appendices
Chef.Leb	19/9/18		9th Bn Royal Innskillings. Northern Boundary of line U.76.74 - Lines with left of Nelson (7th Royal Irish Regt) at U.76.63. Southern Boundary - roughly U.19.b.33.75 - Lines with right of Nelson (2/4th Royal Welsh Fusiliers) at U.19.b.5.10. Company dispositions: B and C Coys - front line, A in support and D in Reserve. Boundary line between front line Coys - Roads U.13.b.35.65. MMy	
do	20/9/18		Th following changes in Company dispositions were made during the night: Subject: Two platoons of A Coy moved from support to front line, and relieved left platoon of B Coy and right platoon of C Coy. The two platoons relieved moved back into support positions in rear of former positions. MMy	
do	21/9/18		Active patrolling carried out during the night. MMy	
do	22/9/18		— do —	O.R.
do	23/9/18		— do — Five Germans gave themselves up to 'C' Coys left Lewis Gun post. Lieut S.E. JONES wounded	O.R.
do	24/9/18		Active patrolling as usual. 2/Lt. A. CONACHER wounded	O.R.
do	25/9/18		'B' Coy carried out a raid at 8pm on the CHATEAU in U.14.c. capturing MMy	2/Lt Cmdg 2/14 Lond R London (Scottish)

WAR DIARY / INTELLIGENCE SUMMARY

2/14th Bn. London Regt (London Scottish)

Army Form C. 2118.

Place	Date	Hour	Summary of Events and Information	Remarks and references to Appendices
Little field	25/9/18 (cont)		I knew of killing 9 Germans & destroying 1 M.G. in post in CHATEAU. Casualties – 1 or Missing 30 & wounded. Battalion was relieved by 2/16th Bon London Regt. & proceeded to BAILLEUL ASYLUM becoming Bath in Brigade Reserve.	Sheet 28 S.W. 1:20000
— do —	26/9/18		No training	O.A.
— do —	27/9/18		Company training and talks during day. Bombed at BAILLEUL. O.R. wounded.	O.A.
— do —	28/9/18 ASYLUM		Company training during morning. Battalion came under orders to move at 1½ hours notice at 6 p.m. Orders to move came in at	O.A.
— do —	29/9/18	11.45 p.m.	Battalion moved off at 1.15 a.m. to march to T.10.a. Hostile aeroplane dropped 5 bombs near Battalion just outside NEUVE EGLISE on WULVERGHEM causing 5 casualties (1 killed and 4 wounded). On arrival at T.10.a. 65.25 Battalion took over under Lodges in both sides spent remaining time in reserve until about 12.30 p.m. when they received orders to go forward and march through 2/16th Lond R. after Battalion had reached MESSINES it	O.A.

Milner Ch
Lt Col Comdg
2/14 Bn R London Regt

2/14th Bn. London Regt.
(London Scottish)

A.F.C. 2118. (5)

WAR DIARY

Summary of Events and Information

Place	Date	Hour	Summary of Events and Information	Remarks and references to Appendices
In the field	29/9/18		was found that the 2/16th Lond.R. had reached their objective the canal in P.20.a. and that the 2/15th Lond.R. and S.LANCS. Regt were on their right. Orders were received that the battalion should take up a line from S.E. along WARNETON – COMINES railway from junction of railway and road at U.12.b.4.5. to junction of railway and road at V.2.b.6.9. This was done in darkness, three companies moving down were moving from O.36.b. to V.1.d. holding in an advance guard, the operation was conducted and companies got into position without incident. Dispositions were as follows:— A' Coy on right from U.12.b.4.5. to V.1.d.3.5. 'D' Coy on left from V.1.a.3.5. to V.2.b.8.9. 'C' Coy in support from O.6.b. 3.3. to P.31.d.4.0. 'B' Coy in reserve in vicinity of Pm.H.R. which was established at O.35.c.6.6.	Sheet 28 1/40000
-do-	30/9/18		When dawn broke WARNETON was found to be occupied by the enemy and T.M. and artillery fire opened. A Coy considerably causing 2 casualties. Brigade on our right had attacked WARNETON at dawn but were could not establish touch with them after 1pm. hostile fire from WARNETON ceased and on pushing out patrols we found it unoccupied. Patrols to the LYS river were fired on from S. bank, and reported all bridges on our front destroyed. During the night 'C' Coy relieved A' Coy	

A.C.L. Smith Lieut.Col.
Comdg 2/14th
London Scottish

2/14th Bn: London Regt
(London Scottish).

WAR DIARY

A.F.C. 2118.

Place	Date	Hour	Summary of Events and Information	Remarks and references to appendices
In the field	30/9/18 (cont)		and 'B' Coy relieved 'D' Coy without incident	a.s
			CASUALTIES for month. KILLED. 2/Lt. R.A. BROWN and 4 O.R. WOUNDED. Lt. S.E. JONES 2/Lt. A. CONACHER } and 45 O.R. MISSING 1 O.R.	
			STRENGTH at end of month 33 Officers 789 O.R.	a.s
			CAPTURES 13 G.huns 3 M.G.'s	a.s

Maybffy Lt Col Comdt
2/14th Lond Regt
London Scottish

REF. SHEET. 28. S.W.
1:20000.

APPENDIX. I.

2/14th Bn. London Regt (London Scottish)
Account of operations of 2nd/3rd Sept. 1918.

The Battalion moved from behind MONT ROUGE as advance guard to the 90th INF. BDE. at 1.15 p.m on 2nd Sept. 1918. The Bgde were to relieve the 21st INF. BDE., who were advancing Eastwards from DRANOUTRE and had reached a line approximately FRENCHMANS FARM N.34.b. 85.40 — N.34.a 30.20 — then S. parallel to and 400 yards E. of DAYLIGHT CORNER — NEUVE EGLISE Road as far as T.9.b.

The Battalion was to relieve the 7th R.I.R. in daylight but this was found to be impracticable so the Battalion was halted at N.31.a 4.5 until dusk. Meanwhile the 7th R.I.R. & 2/23rd Lond. R., who were also in the front line launched another attack, but by the time the battn. had arrived at DAYLIGHT CORNER to relieve, no information had been received regarding the advance. It was thought, however, that little or no progress had been made, so 'D' Coy was detailed to relieve the old line, & take over the whole Bgde. front, but after 2 platoons had gone forward, a report came in that the 2/23rd Lond. R. had taken WULVERGHEM with 3 Coys, who were in an isolated position, & not in touch with either flank. 'A' Coy was sent out to WULVERGHEM to relieve these Coys, whilst 'D' Coy was instructed to advance on to a line approximately from S to N — HILL 35. at T.5.a 8.8. in a N.W direction to FRENCHMANS FARM. This was done without opposition. 'C' Coy were behind 'A' Coy, and advanced towards WULVERGHEM leaving a platoon facing S. as a protective flank, the left post of the next battn. being in T.9.b.

APPENDIX. I (continued)

'B' Coy was behind 'D' Coy

At dawn both front line Coys. advanced with little or no opposition, and finally took up a position as follows from N to S.

'D' Coy. FRENCHMAN'S FARM running E to
VINE CORNER then following S along
track through N.35.a.6.8.d to
T.5.b.20.60. with posts out at
N.35.b.80.75 and N.36.c.1.?

'A' Coy   T.6.a.7.7. to T.6.c.9.8 to T.6.c.5.7.

Both Coys were in touch with their flanks, the battalion on our right having advanced at dawn.

The Supports Coys. also advanced and took up positions as follows

'B' Coy   N.35.c.7.7. to T.5.a.7.8

'C' Coy   in WULVERGHEM with one platoon echeloned back.

B.H.Q.   at N.33.a.72.28.

There were our dispositions during the hours of daylight. At dusk patrols were pushed out eastward, but before any appreciable advance could be made the battalion was relieved by 2/15th Lond. R. and moved back into Reserve at DONEGAL FARM.

CASUALTIES

OTHER RANKS

1 Killed
9 Wounded

Lt Col Cmdg
2/14 Lond. R.
London Scottish

Index..........................

90/30

SUBJECT.

2/14ᵗʰ London Regt.

No.	Contents.	Date.
	October 1918.	

SECRET.

WAR DIARY

OF THE

2/14TH. LONDON (SCOTTISH) REGIMENT

FOR THE MONTH OF

OCTOBER - 1918

(VOLUME 28)

IN THE FIELD.   COMMANDING 2/14TH. LONDON (SCOTTISH) REGT.

* * *

2/14th Bn. London Regt (London Scottish)

WAR DIARY

Army Form C. 2118.

INTELLIGENCE SUMMARY.
(Erase heading not required.)

Place	Date	Hour	Summary of Events and Information	Remarks and references to Appendices
In the field	1/10/18	—	Patrols out to R. LYS again during day. Battalion relieved on night 1st/2nd Oct by 29th D.L.I. 14th Divn. moved into Reserve. Before relief gas shell burst in RAP causing following casualties – CAPT. I.D. STUBBS RAMC Tatts 3/10th LOND.R and 5 O.R. wounded.	Sheet 28 1/40,000
— do —	2/10/18	—	Battalion arrived in Reserve Area at GUN FARM O.27 a.8.8. at about 04.00 hrs	at
— do —	3/10/18	—	Battalion resting, no training. Some shelling but not close	at
— do —	4/10/18	—	D Coy shelled early morning. Casualties 2 O.R. Killed 2 O.R. Died of Wounds 4 O.R. Wounded. Company having carried out during day Specialist training :– Signalling, musketry, scouting, Lewis Gun, Stretcher bearing during afternoon	at
— do —	5/10/18	—	Training as usual	at
— do —	6/10/18	—	No training. General cleaning up.	at
— do —	7/10/18	—	C & D Coys moved to new areas at L'ENFER O.25 d during morning. Usual training.	at
— do —	8/10/18	—	Bathing at WULVERGHEM during morning. Usual training with exception	at

Major Ch. London Scottish
2/14 Lond. R. London Scottish

1/14th London Regt (London Scottish)

Army Form C. 2118.

WAR DIARY
INTELLIGENCE SUMMARY
(Erase heading not required.)

Place	Date	Hour	Summary of Events and Information	Remarks and references to Appendices
In the field	8/10/18		of Scouts. Remainder of Battalion moved to L'ENFER area during afternoon. Bn. H.Q. being established at O.19.d.80.15.	Sheet 28 1/40000
do	9/10/18		Company training in the attack on Open Warfare Principles in Battalion with defended field troops & penetrating through wire. Method deployment in open warfare and the use of the compass for direction through a smoke barrage. Practice in advancing under a barrage at the rate of 100 yards in 2 minutes. Lessons from firing & destruction of machine gun emplacements. Battns. to R DRIVE at WULVERGHEM	
	11/10/18		Relieved 1/5th INNISKILLINGS in the front line taken over on completion from 4th SUSSEX REGT. 101st Bde. Front line from Q.7.c.45 – Q.14.a.2.8. D & C Coy in the line. A & B Coy in reserve and support. Bn HR at A.7.b.85.30. It SANDISON was wounded. Weather fine	
	12/10/18		On the front line. Considerable amount of gas shelling especially in back area	7 AM do
	13/10/18		Taps laid out on jumping off front for the attack, & all necessary preparations made preliminary to attack	7 AM do

2/14th London Regt (London Scottish)

WAR DIARY

Army Form C. 2118.

Place	Date	Hour	Summary of Events and Information	Remarks and references to Appendices
In the field	19/10/18 to 21/10/18		Operations (See Appendix I)	
- do -	22/10/18		In Div Reserve in Billets at TOMBROEK. Kit Inspection, Reorganization and Cleaning up	Shot 29/4/1920
- do -	23/10/18		Coy training, Lewis Gun, Scouting, Signalling Instruction	p.m.
- do -	24/10/18		Coy training, do do. Draft of 115" o.Rs. joined Bn. Lt W.H.MAIR, M.M. to hospital. Bad epidemic of Influenza commenced.	p.m.
- do -	25/10/18		Bathing at ROLLEGHEM. Coy training, Lewis Gun, Scouting and Signalling Instruction	p.m.
- do -	26/10/18		Tactical Scheme carried out by "B" Coy advancing across open country by Sections, close co-operation with Artillery shell section allotted to Bn. Section Commanders carried out open fighting. 2nd Lt J EDGAR to hospital (sick). Influenza Epidemic continues severe. A, C, D Coys carried out Coy Training.	p.m.
- do -	27/10/18		Church Parade, Staff Parade, Inspection of Billets, Inspection of Staff. Football (Cup Series) 2nd London Scottish 3 - 1 (Association) Lt C TENNANT to Hosp (sick)	

(4) Army Form C. 2118.

WAR DIARY
or
INTELLIGENCE SUMMARY

(Erase heading not required.)

1/1st London Regt (London Scottish)

Instructions regarding War Diaries and Intelligence Summaries are contained in F. S. Regs., Part II. and the Staff Manual respectively. Title pages will be prepared in manuscript.

Place	Date	Hour	Summary of Events and Information	Remarks and references to Appendices
In the field	28/10/18		Tactical Scheme by D Coy; advancing over open country, making good by bounds. Co-operation with Artillery. Practice of Communications. Reinforcements. Officers (A & S.M.) Journal. Bn. A.B.C Coys carried out Coy Training	Sheet 29 issued
- do -	29/10/18		Tactical Scheme by A Coy. Co-operation with Artillery practised. Reinforcements at BOLLEGHEM. BCD Coys carried out Coy Training. Journal of Bn Inter-Coy Football. D Coy 3 goals — C Coy nil. Event by 3rd Div Forest Patl.	8 P.M. 7 P.M. 7 P.M.
- do -	30/10/18		Company training. Sents & Signallers.	Event by 3rd Div Forest Patl Tactical Scheme by "C" Coy 7 P.M.
- do -	31/10/18		Company training. Specialist training. Scouts, Signallers. Range taken.	1 P.M.

[signature]
Major Comdg
1/14 London R
London Scottish

Appendix I
Operations. 14th - 21st October.

Ref map
Sheet 28
Sheet 29 1/40000

14th

At 04.30. Bn. H.Q. moved to T.8.c.

At 05.35 on 14th Oct. Bn advanced to the attack.

The objective was line of road in Q.22.a. Quest Farm. Road junction Q.17.c.2.2. 2/15 London Regt attacked on right. 101st Inf. Bde. 7. Cheshires left.

The Bn. advanced on a 2 Company front. "D" on right "C" on left with "B" Coy in support. "A" in reserve.

The attack was carried out under cover of a creeping barrage which lifted 100 yards every two minutes. A considerable smoke barrage was also put down.

The Bn. at the start met with a considerable amount of M.G. fire and warm resistance from defended pill boxes. The leading Coys. pressed on however and the Support Coy. dealt with any pill boxes and defended localities which had not already been dealt with.

The smoke barrage although making direction difficult assisted the attacking Coys. materially and considerably reduced casualties as the front wave was on the enemy before he had time to realise what was happening.

Objectives were taken by 07.35 and consolidation commenced. The barrage was excellent and opposition met with was chiefly M.G.s from defended pill boxes.

Casualties were about 20% of the attacking and support Coys. 220 prisoners were taken and a large number of the enemy were killed.

Lieut. H/My Smith & 2nd Lieut. Cotton were wounded. 16 O.R.s were killed and 43 wounded.

A number of enemy M.G.s & T.M.s were captured. Also a considerable amount of booty including 5 Railway trucks.

Patrols were immediately sent out. These were heavily shelled and ascertained that enemy were established in defensive line about 500 yards distant.

15th

Continued to hold line of objective which was organised in depth and pushed forward patrols to clear up situation in front.

At dusk enemy retired from line of railway in 2.21 and 2.22. ~~We followed up and took up a line along this railway. Bn. H.Q. moving Q.16.d.2.3.~~ "C" + "D" remained in front line. "A" Coy.

Coy relieved "B" in support the latter Coy becoming Bn Reserve.

During the night 15/16th the enemy evacuated area N. of LYS on our front. Patrols of 2/15th London Regt. on our right reached LYS N. of BOUSBECQUE. Brigade on our left entered MENIN.

Posts were established along line MENIN-BATTOM CROSS ROAD from which the whole of R. LYS could be commanded to the front.

Patrols were sent forward to R. LYS and hostile M.G.s encountered firing from E. side of river from vicinity of FACTORIES BRIDGE and R.19.C.2.3. The bridges on our front were found to have been destroyed.

16th

"A" Coy relieved "C" & "D" Coys in the front line the latter two Coys moving into support.

17th

Enemy retreated from LYS and 2/15th London Regt. followed up on the right crossing the river at BOUSBECQUE & 2/16th on the left crossed the river at MENIN. The R.E.s having constructed pontoon bridges. 2/15th London Regt. & 2/16th made good line of high ground W.5.d.3.5. — W.6.b. — R.31.a. HALLUIN (incl.) — LYS at R.16.C.8.0.

At dusk 2/15th London Regt. pushed on and took up a line E. of RONCQ and BN. followed in support crossing river at BOUSBECQUE & proceeded to RONCQ. where BN. remained during the night of 17th/18th in billets.

The situation at the close of the day was "The enemy had retreated. The 90th Inf. Bde. held the line RONCQ. MONT D'HALLUIN RECKEM. in touch with 31 DIV. on right at RONCQ and 34 DIV in RECKEM."

18th

The Brigade advanced on a two BN. front. 2/14th London Regt. on right. 2/16th on left.

The boundary for the BN. was on the North E & W. grid line between R.29 and R.35 on the South RONCQ (exc) MONT D'HALLUIN (incl) STERHOEK (inc). The BN. passed through 2/15th at 06.30 and took up position on a line N & S DRONKAARD (R.35.d) RECKEM within BN boundaries by 07.15

Within BN. boundaries the first objective was N & S grid line M.20. 26. 32 S.2

The second objective was MOUSCRON-KNOCK RLY
" third " " STERHOEK-PRESHOEK-KNOCK
"B" formed Advanced Guard "C" left support "D" right support "A" in

in reserve.

The 10th H.L.I. 31st Div. were on our right. The first objective was taken without opposition by 10·00.

Second objective was reached 12·30. Enemy M.G. fire and shelling was met with during advance to second objective and advance guard was unable for some hours to cross railway owing to enfilade M.G. fire from vicinity of STERHOEK TILE WORKS and to fact that right flank was in the air owing to non arrival of Bn on right.

Bn. H.Q. moved to M.32.d.1.6.

At 15.00 hrs advance guard pushed over the railway meeting with considerable M.G. fire and shelling from high ground in immediate front and established outposts over ridge in front of road running from M.28.d.3.6 to M.34.d.7.4 thence back to railway.

Advanced Guard Coy could not advance beyond this line owing to right flank being entirely exposed and considerable M.G. fire from right flank from vicinity of STERHOEK TILE WORKS which enfiladed the whole line.

At dusk "D" Coy in right support made a demonstration with the intention of clearing up the situation on the right flank the 10th H.L.I. not yet having come up in line. This was successful and enemy M.G's withdrew to another position further back.

19th

At 02·00 "C" Coy went through "B" Coy who withdrew to billets, and under cover of an artillery barrage made good the line STERHOEK-AELBEKE Road. Patrols were then sent out to TOLPENHOEK and high ground N.36.central and outposts established. Considerable opposition from enemy M.G's was met with.

By 1730 on 18th 10th H.L.I. had reached line of the railway on our right but there was a gap of 500 yards which "D" Coy. filled with one platoon.

During the night the enemy retreated.

At 08·00 the Bn continued the advance and was allotted further objectives.

4.

Bn. Boundaries were as follows -

S. Boundary on straight line from BOUSBECQUE au TRIEU
des PREPRES - MOUSCRON (exc) - CROMBION (exc)
DOTTIGNIES (exc) to Canal de L'ESCAUT or L'ENFER.

N. Boundary STERHOEK - TOLPENHOEK Road.
M.35.c.3.2 to S.5.b.6.6 (exc) - ZEVECOTEN T.7a (inc).
FME HERBAI T.18d (inc).

The Brigade group advanced on a two Bn. front 2/16
on left London Scottish on the right.

The 20th Middlesex 43rd Bde were on our right. "A" Coy
formed Advance Guard "D" right support "B" left support
"C" in reserve.

Advance was carried out as follows -

1st Objective. High ground in S.10.
2nd   "   The line Le Compas S.18a - ZEVECOTEN T.7a
3rd   "   The line PETIT VOISINAGE (T.19.b) exc
             TOMBROEK - FM HERBAI T.8.d.

?13.45 All objectives were gained by 01.45 without opposition.
Fresh orders were received to push on to -

T.28.b   4th Objective. PONT D'AVIS T.18.b.1.8. along road to
                         T.16.a.4.7.
          5th   "   line Dottignies - GEUZENHOEK within the
                         Bn. Boundaries.

The 4th Objective was taken with slight opposition from
snipers and M.G. fire.

Owing to the fact that both flanks were exposed
especially the left the 2/16 London Regt having met
considerable opposition from enemy M.G's and to the fact
that enemy held the high ground in vicinity of PETIT
TOURCOING it was not possible to gain 5th objective.

An outpost line was therefore established for the night on
the line of the 4th Objective.

Patrols were sent out and by dawn reported that enemy had
retired.

20th
     The Bn continued the advance at 07.30 covering

the 90th Bde group. 20th Middlesex 43 Bde were on
our right. 116th Cheshires 21st Bde were on our left.
"D" Coy formed Advanced Guard "C" Coy Right Support
"B" Coy Left Support "A" in reserve.

Boundaries were:-

N. TOMBROEK (inc) COYGHEM (inc) HELCHIN (exc)
S. CROMBION (exc) DOTTINGIES (exc) L'ENFER
37 C.30 (inc)

Bn advanced by bounds as follows:-

1st Objective.
    Road T.29a thence Road T.17.c

2nd Objective
    Road T.29d - T.24.c - T.24.a.

3rd Objective
    Railway about 37.O.1.a.9.7. thence road to
    COYGHEM.

4th Objective 37.O.2.b central. PIJPISTRAAT. CITADEL
                                            U.26.b.

5th and Final Objective
    ESPIERRES - HELCHIN ROAD.

The 3rd Objective was reached at 13.25 without much
opposition. On arrival on this objective enemy opened vigorous
shelling on left of our line in vicinity of COYGHEM.
Lieut. S.A. Paterson was wounded and the left was hung
up for some hours.

By this time 20th Middlesex had got well forward
on the right but Cheshires were hung up along line of
COYGHEM - RUDDERVOORDE ROAD by enemy who were
holding high ground in T.20. and T.14 in strength.

Advanced Guard however pushed on and gained 4th
objective but could proceed no further until the light failed.

At dusk they pushed on towards final objective ie line
of road ESPIERRES - HELCHIN.

By 2200 hours patrols of advanced guard reached 5th objective, but the line of this objective was not made good owing to the fact that left flank was completely in the air. The 20th Middlesex were along line of river on our immediate right but the Cheshires kept right post was W. of U 26 b 8. 8. The following outpost line was therefore established with our left flank thrown back to keep touch with the Cheshires Liaison Post C 3 d 3. 2 with 20th Middlesex Outpost Line C 3 d 7 5 — U 27 d 3. 6 B Coy forming a defensive flank along the general line U 27 c 6.6 — U 26 b 8. 9 — TROIS FM.

21st. At 05.30 Cheshires attacked on the left and by 1230 had taken HELCHIN thereby clearing up the situation on our left. During the afternoon the 2/17th Lond R. passed through our line and Bn withdrew to billets at TOM BROEK

The total Casualties during the operations 11th — 21st October were

    4 Officers wounded
 22 OR's Killed
 73 OR's wounded

                              JM.

Total Bn Strength   41 Officers   764 OR's

With Bn   25 Officers   539 OR's
Away from Bn   16   225
                     41   764
                              not including Chaplain

Detail away	Offrs	OR
Field Amb	6	92
Offrs Rest Camp	1	1
Leave	5	70
Mil. Duty	—	13
F.P. Camp	—	1
Command	3	28
Courses	—	17
Detachment	1	3
	16	225

Army Form W.3091.

Cover for Documents.

Nature of Enclosures.

CONFIDENTIAL.

WAR   DIARY

of the

2/14th. Bn. London Regiment
(London Scottish)

for the month of

NOVEMBER   1918.

In the Field.
4/12/18.

Major.
Comdg. 2/14 London Regiment
(London Scottish)

Notes, or Letters written.

2/14th.Bn.London Regiment London Scottish

A.F. C. 2118

W A R D I A R Y.

Sheet 29
1/40000

In the Field.	
1/11/18.	The Battalion received order to move, and on the night of the 1st-2nd. left TOMBROEK and 500x over a part of the line along the Bank of the River ESCAUT V.9.c.2.9. to P.34.C.7.5. from the 16th.Bn.Cheshire Regiment. The 2/16th.Lond.R. were on our right and the 2/15th.Bn.Lond.R. on the left. A. & B Coys were in the line C & D Coys in support. The relief was carried out without incident.
2/11/18.	The day was uneventful. Movement was restricted on out part as the enemy had excellent observation from the high ground Mount d'ENGLUS immediately on our front. There was occasional fire from enemy machine guns and trench mortars throughout the day. During the night 2nd. 3rd. patrols from A. & B Coys were active along the river bank with the object of reconnoitring for a suitable crossing on our front.
3/11/18.	During the day the enemy's artillery was very active along the front and a considerable amount of gas was used. We had no casualties. On the night of the 3rd 4th. C & D Coys relieved A & B who went into support. Patrols from C & D Coys were very active during the night but failed to cross the river. The river on our front was unfordable and bridging materials arrived too late to be of use that night.
4/11/18.	Enemy artillery again active. The village of AVELGHEM was heavily shelled and the church set on fire. C.Coy. had two O.R. killed and 5 wounded. On the night 4th-5th. the Bn. was relieved. The right coy. front was taken over by the 2/16th.Lond.R. and our left coy. from the 7/8th.Bn. R. Innis.Fus. The relief was conducted without incident. The Bn. moved back to billets at GEUZENHOEK T.f.a. that night.
5/11/18.	The Battalion was ordered to move to billets at BELLEGHEM N.27. but the order was cancelled. Cleaning up during morning.
6/11/18.	Under fresh instructions the Bn. moved to Billets at MARRIONETTE near St.ANNE.
7/11/18.	The Bn. occupied the area N.14. Coy. training was carried out during the morning; Lewis Gun, Scouting, Signalling instruction etc., Lt.Col. R.J.L.Ogilby.D.S.O. rejoined the Bn. from Leave
8/11/18.	Coy. route marches during the morning and cleaning up.
9/11/18.	Bn. proceeded to MOEN. U.f.h. Enemy retired from his position along east bank of River ESCAUT. A Coy. sent forward to assist engineers in bridging river at ESCANAFFLES
10/11/18.	A.Coy. went into Billets at AVELGHEM. B & C Coys. moved up and D.Coy. worked with R.E. at bridging.
11/11/18.	Hostilities ceased at 1100. C.Coy. relieved B. and finished bridging the river with R.E.
12/11/18.	H.Q. and D. Coy. moved to AVELGHEM joining the other 3 Coys. there. Coy. Training including practice March Past.
13/11/18.	Training by Coys. as before. Captain.M.R.Mitchell proceeded on leave to England.
14/11/18.	Paper chase carried out in Morning. Bn. played 2/16th.Lond.R. at Rugby Football in afternoon. No score.
15/11/18.	Bn. Moved to billets at MARRIONETTE N.14.a.

In the Field 16/11/18.	Coy. training in close order drill. Cleaning up generally
17/11/18.	Thanksgiving Service at ST.ANNE.N.10.a. Capt.I.D.STUBBS. R.A.M.C. att 2/14th.L.R. rejoined from Hospital in place of Captain.G.MACDONALD. R.A.M.C. 2/Lt.C.J.JACKSON and 2/Lt. D.T.McPherson rejoined Bn.from leave.
18/11/18.	Coy. training in close order drill etc.
19/11/18.	Coy. route marches in morning. Lt.S.G.WILSON proceeded on special leave to England. 2/Lts. E.P.BRAY and J.P.DONALD joined Bn. Capt.I.D.STUBBS. R.A.M.C. att. 2/14th. Lond.R. proceeded to Hospital
20/11/18.	Coy. training as before in close order drill etc. Capt.C.R.RECKITTS. R.A.M.C. joined Bn.
21/11/18.	Battalion Ceremonial Parade in Morning. Lt.E.CAMERON Cameron Hldrs. att. 2/14th .Lond. R.Proceeded to Hospital. Football London Scottish V Queens Westminster Rifled .Result 3 - 2.
22/11/18.	Bn. Parade practice Ceremonial drill.
23/11/18.	Bn. Parade practice ceremonial drill, march past etc. Football London Scottish V 98th . Field Ambulance. Result 1 - 0.
24/11/18.	Church Services in morning. 2/Lt.B.W.Adams proceeded on leave to France.
25/11/18.	Bn. Parade practice ceremonial drill
26/11/18.	Brigade Parade for presentation of medals, by Major-General W.de L. Williams C.M.G. D.S.O. Captain.Robertson.M.C. awarded Par to M.C. military Crosses awarded to Capt. W. Anderson D.C.M., Lt.P.Geddes., Lt.C.Tennant., and 2/Lt.C.J.McIndoor.
27/11/18.	Inter-Platoon Cross Country Runs by Coys. in morning
28/11/18.	Coy. training ,Lewis Gun,Signalling, etc.,
29/11/18.	Platoon training. Lt.Col.R.J.Ogilby.D.S.O. and Captain J.S.Monro proceeded on leave in France. Association Football Match Divisional Knockout Competition Queens Westminster V London Scottish Result 4 - 3.
30/11/18	Bn. moved as part of Brigade column from MARRIONETTE to LINSELLES Area by General Route ST. ANNE Road Junction N.18.c.8.1./ AELBEKE /VIELLEMOTTE Cross-roads/ NEUVILLE / Road Junction ¼ mile W. of V of VILLHOF/ Road Junction ½ mile N. of L OF LES ORIONS / Road Junction ½ mile W. of V of VILLHOF TO / LA ROUSSERIE/ LA VIGNETTE. Bn. was billetted in LA VIGNETTE . Ref. maps. Belgium and France Sheet. 29 1/40000 . TOURNAI 5.

4/12/18.

Comdg. 2/14th.London Regiment
Major.
(London Scottish)

Army Form W.3091.

Cover for Documents.

Nature of Enclosures.

CONFIDENTIAL

2/14th. Bn. London Regiment. (London Scottish)

W A R   D I A R Y

for

the month of

D E C E M B E R   1918.

Lieut.-Colonel.
Comdg. 2/14th. Bn. London Regiment.
(London Scottish)

Notes, or Letters written.

2/14 O. London Regt. (London Irish)

WAR DIARY
or
INTELLIGENCE SUMMARY.
(Erase heading not required.)

Army Form C. 2118.

Place	Date	Hour	Summary of Events and Information	Remarks and references to Appendices
In the field	1/12/18		Ref. maps:- TOURNAI 5", 1/100,000. HAZEBROUCK 5a, 1/100,000. Bn. moved as part of Bde. column from LA VIGNETTE to CROIX au BOIS by general route:- LINSELLES — QUESNOY — CROIX au BOIS and billeted for night 1/2nd December in old huts.	Ay
	2/12/18		Bn. continued move as part of Bde column from CROIX au BOIS to LA GORGUE by general route:- FONQUEREAU — LA PREVOTE — LA PREVOTE FRELING- HIEN road — HOUPLINES — ARMENTIERES — ERQUINGHEM — SAILLY-SUR-LA-LYS — ESTAIRES — LAGORGUE and was billeted for night 2nd/3rd December in LAGORGUE	Ay
	3/12/18		Bn. continued move as part of Bde column from LA GORGUE to ST VENANT by general route:- Road junction S. of MERVILLE STATION — CALONNE — SUR- LA-LYS — ST FLORIS — ST VENANT and was billeted for night 3/4. December in empty asylum	Ay
	4/12/18		Bn. continued move as part of Bde column from ST VENANT to LES CISEAUX by general route:- HAVERSKERQUE — CROIX MARRAISSE — LE FORET — TANNAY — THIENNES — BOESEGHEM, and were billeted in LES CISEAUX and LACARNOIS	Ay

Murphy
Lt. Col.
Commanding 2/14 London Regt (London Irish)

WAR DIARY or INTELLIGENCE SUMMARY

Army Form C. 2118.

2/14 London Regt (London Scottish)

Place	Date	Hour	Summary of Events and Information	Remarks and references to Appendices
LES CISEAUX	5/12/18		Coys at disposal of Coy Commanders for general cleaning up and interior economy. Afternoon devoted to improvement of billets.	pd
	6/12/18		3 hours training. Lewis gun, signalling, N.C.O. class, physical training. Class afternoon devoted to games and inter platoon station football begun.	pd
	7/12/18		Boy route marches 9 miles. Afternoon games and football. Award of French decorations awarded, notified :— CROIX de GUERRE a l'ordre CORPS. CAPT. + ADJT. J.S. MONRO. do DIVISION. C.S.M. J.G. HORNE "B" Coy. No 510222 do REGIMENT PTE. A. O'BRIEN C 510637	pd
	8/12/18		Voluntary Church Services. Presbyterian and Roman Catholic at BOESEGHEM Church of England at LES CISEAUX	pd
	9/12/18		"A" + "D" Coys dismantling defences in LES CISEAUX area. Afternoon games and football league. "B" and "C" Coys moved to huts at I.32.b 30.75. Refmap Sheet 36A 1/40,000	pd
LES CISEAUX and LA LACQUE	10/12/18		All Coys dismantling defences in respective areas. Afternoon games and football league	pd

(signed) J Moseley
2/Lt
Comdg 2/14 London Regt (London Scottish)

WAR DIARY
INTELLIGENCE SUMMARY

Army Form C. 2118.

2/4th London Regt (London Scottish)

Place	Date	Hour	Summary of Events and Information	Remarks and references to Appendices
LES CISEAUX and LALACQUE	11/12/18		"A" & "D" boys. Route march 8 miles. "B" and "C" boys dismantling defences of afternoon:- games and football league	p.j.
	12/12/18		"B" & "C" boys Route march 8 miles. "A" & "D" boys dismantling defences. Afternoon:- games and football league	p.j.
	13/12/18		"A" & "D" boys dismantling defences. "B" & "C" boys. Coy drill and kit inspection. Afternoon:- games and football league.	p.j.
	14/12/18		"A" & "D" boys Coy drill and kit inspection. "B" & "C" boys dismantling defences.	p.j.
	15/12/18		Voluntary Church services at BOESEGHEM and LALACQUE	p.j.
	16/12/18		"A" & "D" boys Route march 8 miles. "B" & "C" boys dismantling defences. Afternoon:- games and football league.	p.j.
	17/12/18		Bn less "C" Coy attended Bn ceremonial parade near PONT de THIENNES (Ref. map Sheet 36a 1/20,000 when French Decorations as notified in ? Dec 1918 were presented by Brig. Genl. G.A. STEVENS D.S.O. "C" Coy dismantling defences. Afternoon:- games and football	p.j.

M Moseley Lt Col

Comdg 2/4th London Regt (London Scottish)

2/14 London Regt (London Scottish)

WAR DIARY
or
INTELLIGENCE SUMMARY.
(Erase heading not required.)

Army Form C. 2118.

Instructions regarding War Diaries and Intelligence Summaries are contained in F. S. Regs., Part II. and the Staff Manual respectively. Title pages will be prepared in manuscript.

Place	Date	Hour	Summary of Events and Information	Remarks and references to Appendices
LES CISEAUX and LA CLAQUE	18/12/18		"A" & "D" Coys route march 8 miles. "B" & "C" Coy dismantling defences afternoon. - Games and football league	fl.
	19/12/18		"A" & "D" Coys Platoon drill. "B" Coy dismantling defences. "C" Coy wiring and afternoon	fl
	20/12/18		P. of W. escort parties for new camp. afternoon - Games & football league. "A" & "D" Coys dismantling defences. "C" Coy Platoon Drill. "B" Coy wiring and	fl
	21/12/18		P. of W. escort parties for new camp. afternoon Games & football league. "A" & "D" Coys Company Drill and Kit Inspection. "B" & "C" Coys & Q.M. move into new camp at LA CLAQUE. afternoon. - Games and football league	fl
	22/12/18		Voluntary Church service at DOESEGHEM and LA CLAQUE. afternoon.-	fl
	(23/12/18)		Rugby & football match. 30th DIV. artillery v 2/14 INF. BDE. Recruits platoons	fl
	23/12/18		"A" & "D" Coys move to new camp at LA CLAQUE. "B" and "C" Coys work on new camp.	fl
LA CLAQUE	24/12/18		All Coys. Work in camp. afternoon. Games and football league.	fl
	25/12/18		Church Parade. Christmas festivities.	fl
	26/12/18		Inter-company tournament (Rugby)	fl
	27/12/18		Company route march. Games and football league.	fl

Army Form C. 2118.

1/1th London Regt (London Scottish)

WAR DIARY
or
INTELLIGENCE SUMMARY.
(Erase heading not required.)

Instructions regarding War Diaries and Intelligence Summaries are contained in F. S. Regs., Part II. and the Staff Manual respectively. Title pages will be prepared in manuscript.

Place	Date	Hour	Summary of Events and Information	Remarks and references to Appendices
LA CROSSE	28/12/16		Company kit inspection and Interior Economy officers + names further North Trenches.	ff
	29/12/16			ff
	30/12/16		"A" + "B" Coys dismantling defences "C" + "D" Coys Coy training signalling and route marches. offence bomb games and further signal.	ff
	31/12/16		"A" + "B" Coys Coy training "C" + "D" Coys dismantling defences signalling + route marches	ff
			Note:– Average classification from 1st to 31st December Ration Strength – 691	

My (signature)
Lt-Col
comdg 1/14 London Regt
(London Scottish)

Army Form W.3091.

Cover for Documents.

Nature of Enclosures.

CONFIDENTIAL

WAR DIARY

For the month of

JANUARY 1919.

2/14th. Bn. London Regiment (London Scottish)

Major.
Comdg. 2/14th. Bn. London Regiment
(London Scottish)

1/2/19.

Notes, or Letters written.

2/14 Bn. London Regt.
(London Scottish)

Army Form C. 2118.

WAR DIARY
INTELLIGENCE SUMMARY

(Erase heading not required.)

Ref maps:- HAZEBROUCK 1/100,000
CALAIS 1/100,000

Place	Date	Hour	Summary of Events and Information	Remarks and references to Appendices
			Education	
LA LACQUE	1-1-19		Boys at disposal of Bn. Comdr. clearing up & preparing for move places	P.J.
	2-1-19		Coy drill. Signalling & Lewis Gun classes. Afternoon football.	P.J.
In the field	3-1-19		Bn. moved to COYECQUE by the general route AIRE - MAMETZ - THEROUANNE - DELETTE - COYECQUE and billeted for night 3/4th Jan in the village & huts	do P.J.
	4-1-19		Bn. moved to HERLY by the general route FAUQUEMBERGUES - RENTY - VERCHOCQ - HERLY and occupied huts for night 4/5th Jan.	P.J.
	5-1-19		Bn. moved to MONTCAVREL area, H.Q. and 2 Coys to ESTREE and ESTRELLES and 2 Coys to RECQUES by the general route AVESNES - MANINGHEM - REMORTIER - LA MOTTE - CLENLEU - ALETTE - MONTCAVREL, and billeted for night 5/6. Jan. in villages.	P.J.
	6-1-19		Bn. moved to ETAPLES area by general route ESTREE - NEUVILLE - ATTIN - BEUTIN - ENOCQ - ETAPLES and occupied huts in camp of No. 6 Convalescent Depot	P.J.
ETAPLES	7-1-19		Coy and Platoon drill. Afternoon football, hockey.	P.J.
	8-1-19		Physical Trg. & Platoon drill. do	P.J.
	9-1-19		Coy route marches. Skeletonworks. do	

J. Lindsay Major
Comdg 2/14 London Regt.
(London Scottish)

Army Form C. 2118.

WAR DIARY
INTELLIGENCE SUMMARY.
(Erase heading not required.)

2/14 Bn London Regt
(London Scottish)

Instructions regarding War Diaries and Intelligence Summaries are contained in F. S. Regs., Part II. and the Staff Manual respectively. Title pages will be prepared in manuscript.

Place	Date	Hour	Summary of Events and Information	Remarks and references to Appendices
ETAPLES	10.1.19		Physical drill. Wearing lewis guns and 2 equipment. Afternoon games. Education classes	P.J
	11.1.19		do. and return training. Baths.	do
	12.1.19		Church services. Camp Inspection.	P.J
	13.1.19		Physical and bay drill. Baths taken over. Guards & Piquets in area.	do
	14.1.19		do. Guards & Piquets. Afternoon games.	do
	15.1.19		Battn moved into new camp in ETAPLES area during day	JJ
	16.1.19		Arrangement of new camp. Guards & Piquets.	JJ
	17.1.19		Physical drill. Coy training and bathing parades. Hockey in afternoon	
	18.1.19		Company drill. Guards & Piquets. Educational classes.	
	19.1.19		Church services. Camp Inspection. Capt W. ANDERSON MC DCM rejoined from leave.	JJ
	20.1.19		Physical training. Coy drill. Afternoon football. Educational classes	JJ
	21.1.19		Battn route march. Guards & Piquets etc.	JJ
	22.1.19		Physical training. Coy drill. Guards & Piquets. Educational classes.	JJ
	23.1.19		do. Educational classes. Capt J. Monro proceeded on leave to U.K.	

J. D. Ryrie Major
Comdg 2/14 London Regt
(London Scottish)

2/14 London Regt
London Scottish

Army Form C. 2118.

WAR DIARY
or
INTELLIGENCE SUMMARY.
(Erase heading not required.)

Instructions regarding War Diaries and Intelligence Summaries are contained in F. S. Regs., Part II. and the Staff Manual respectively. Title pages will be prepared in manuscript.

Place	Date	Hour	Summary of Events and Information	Remarks and references to Appendices
ETAPLES	24.1.19		Battn Route March. Guards Piquet. Football in afternoon.	fg
	25.1.19		Physical Training and Company drill. Educational Classes	fg
	26.1.19		Church services and camp inspection. 2/Lieut R.C. GRAHAM rejoined	fg
			Battn from leave	
	27.1.19		Physical Training + Company drill. Educational Classes 2/LIEUT J GLOVER	fg
			rejoined Battn from leave	
	28.1.19		Battn route march. Games	fg
	29.1.19		Physical drill + company training. Guards Piquets. Educational classes	fg
	30.1.19		do do	fg
	31.1.19		Battn route march. Guards Piquet. Hockey in afternoon	fg
			Total number of officers and men demobilised during	
			the month. Officers 4 Men 209	
			Ration Strength: 20 Officers + 71 O.R.	

Q.R. Lee
Major
(Comdg 2/14 Bn London Regt
London Scottish)

Secret

Army Form W.3091.

Cover for Documents.

Nature of Enclosures.

2/14TH. BN. LONDON REGIMENT.

(LONDON SCOTTISH).

W A R   D I A R Y.

FOR MONTH ENDING.   FEBRUARY 1919.

A. Whyte
Major.
2/14th Bn. London Regiment.
(LONDON SCOTTISH).

Notes, or Letters written.

1/14 London Reg't (London Scottish)

WAR DIARY
INTELLIGENCE SUMMARY

Army Form C. 2118.

FEB. 1919

(Erase heading not required.)

Instructions regarding War Diaries and Intelligence Summaries are contained in F. S. Regs., Part II. and the Staff Manual respectively. Title pages will be prepared in manuscript.

Place	Date	Hour	Summary of Events and Information	Remarks and references to Appendices
ETAPLES	1.2.19		Washing Clothes — Education — Guards & duties	
	2.2.19		Voluntary Church Parades — Presbyterian in Scottish Church Hut. — C of E in Military Church. — R.C. in C of E Church. — Guards.	
	3.2.19		Church Parade of C.E. held preceded by U.K. equipment. Physical Training, Coy Training, Education.	
	4.2.19		Washing Parade — Guards.	
	5.2.19		Physical Training — Coy Training — Education	
	6.2.19		Cleaning Camp during morning. — Guards & duties	
			Batt. MOVED to LE GOUFFRE CAMP. (afternoon)	
LE GOUFFRE	7.2.19		Route march during morning. Working on new Camp	
	8.2.19		Platoon football (afternoon)	
			Coy Training (including Run.) — Education — Kit inspection — Camp gradually resettled.	
	9.2.19		Camp Inspection — Guards & duties	
	10.2.19		Coy Training — do — (At night Madam Wallings Concert Party)	
	11.2.19		Coy Training — Guards & duties — London Scottish Concert party performed at night	
	12.2.19		Drafts from 1/14 London arrived. — do — To Officers & 200 Other Ranks Uniform, London Scottish, & Oxfords +	
	13.2.19		Queen's Triumph. 2 Goals. — Guards & duties.	
	14.2.19		Coy Training — do —	

Cmdg. 1/14 London Regiment
(London Scottish)
Major.

Army Form C. 2118.

2/14 London Reg't (London Scottish)

WAR DIARY
INTELLIGENCE SUMMARY
(Erase heading not required.)

Instructions regarding War Diaries and Intelligence Summaries are contained in F. S. Regs., Part II. and the Staff Manual respectively. Title pages will be prepared in manuscript.

Place	Date	Hour	Summary of Events and Information	Remarks and references to Appendices
LE GOUFFRE	15-2-19		Coy training — Kit inspection — Guards & duties.	
"	16.2.19		Voluntary Church Service (Rev. J. Elliott) — Camp inspection — Guards & duties.	
"	17.2.19		Coy training — NCO's parade under RSM. — Guards & duties.	
"	18.2.19		Route march — Guards & duties — Inter Coy football (afternoon) "A" Coy v. "C" Coy 2.	
"	19.2.19		Coy training — NCO's parade under RSM — Education — Guards & duties	
"	20.2.19		do do do	
"	21.2.19		Inter Coy football (afternoon) D Coy 2 C Coy 1.	
"			Route march — Platoon football (afternoon)	
"	22.2.19		Coy training — Kit inspection — Bathing.	
"	23.2.19		Voluntary Church Service (Rev. J. Elliott) — Camp inspection — Guards & duties — Football Inter Coy League (afternoon) A Coy 2 D Coy 0.	
"	24.2.19		Coy training — Specialist training Carried out:- Lewis Gunners, Signallers, Stretcher bearers — NCO's parade under RSM.	
"	25.2.19		Guards & duties — Coy training — Guards & duties.	
"	26.2.19		Lewis Gun training — NCO's parade under RSM. — Signalling class.	

G.I. Wade 2/Lt. for Major
Comdg 2/14 Bn London Regt
(London Scottish)

2/1st London Regt (London Scottish)

Army Form C. 2118.

WAR DIARY
of
INTELLIGENCE SUMMARY.
(Erase heading not required.)

Instructions regarding War Diaries and Intelligence Summaries are contained in F. S. Regs., Part II. and the Staff Manual respectively. Title pages will be prepared in manuscript.

Place	Date	Hour	Summary of Events and Information	Remarks and references to Appendices
LE GOUFFRE	26.2.19 (cont'd)		Education — Guards & duties — Football (afternoon) Inter-Coy league.	
"	27.2.19		D Coy 1. A Coy O. Levée Sur Sarong — NCO's (Corporals) under R.S.M. — Signalling class — Guards & duties. Motor football. — Running (afternoon)	
"	28.2.19		Coy training (including Kit inspection) — Signalling class — Lg training. Guards & duties — afternoon, Etaples & Aubriet Cross Country run; Runners:-	
"			De 2.1. 1st London Scottish 2nd; Warwicks 3rd; 1/4 London (attached London Scottish) 4th; London Scottish (3rd team) 5th. (Eight other ranks ran). Ration Strength. 24 Officers. 337 Other Ranks.	

A. White Major
Comdg 2/1 Bn London Regt
(London Scottish).

SECRET.

WAR DIARY

OF THE

2/14th. LONDON REGIMENT

FOR THE MONTH OF

MARCH 1919

ETAPLES
5-4-19.

Lt-Col.
Commanding 2/14th. Battalion London Regiment.
(London Scottish.)

2/14 LONDON REG.T
(LONDON SCOTTISH)

Army Form C. 2118.

WAR DIARY
or
INTELLIGENCE SUMMARY.
(Erase heading not required.)

Place	Date	Hour	Summary of Events and Information	Remarks and references to Appendices
LE COUFFRE (LE TOUQUET)	1-3-19		Coy training — Bathing parade — Duties Y.P. Compound (ETAPLES) —	61
	2.3.19		Afternoon:- Inter-Coy League. "D" # "C" 2. Voluntary Church Service (Rev J. Collerell) — Camp Inspection — Duties as on the 1st.	61
	3.3.19		Afternoon:- LONDON SCOTTISH 2. MACHINE GUN CORPS 0. Coy training — NCO's class under R.S.M.	61
	4.3.19		Coy training — Bathing parade — R.S.M's class	61
	5.3.19		Afternoon:- Football Inter-Coy League. "A" 2 "C" 0. Coy training — NCO's class under R.S.M. — Educational classes	61
	6.3.19		Physical & Coy training — NCO's class & Educational classes as on 5th inst.	61
	7.3.19		Training as on the 6th inst with following additions:- Blanket disinfection	61
	8.3.19		Bathing parade (afternoon) Physical & Coy training — R.S.M's class — Kit Inspection — Evening:- Batt. dance held in the Lewis Gun School Theatre (members of the A.M.A.A.C. Corps invited)	61
	9.3.19		Divine Service held in Camp. Camp Inspection — Afternoon — Football. London Scottish 2. M.G.C. 0.	61

2/14 London Regiment.
(The London Scottish)

Army Form C. 2118.

WAR DIARY
or
INTELLIGENCE SUMMARY.
(Erase heading not required.)

Instructions regarding War Diaries and Intelligence Summaries are contained in F.S. Regs., Part II. and the Staff Manual respectively. Title pages will be prepared in manuscript.

Place	Date	Hour	Summary of Events and Information	Remarks and references to Appendices
Le Gouffre	10.3.19		Company training — Cleaning Camp.	61
(Le Touquet)	11.3.19		do — Bathing & washing Parades	62
"	12.3.19		Physical training — Coy training — Afternoon, Football. London Scottish 4 goals	62
"			Oxford & Bucks Bn. 1 goal. (On Golf Links Ground.)	62
"	13.3.19		Physical & Company training.	62
"	14.3.19		Physical & Company training. — Cleaning Camp	62
"	15.3.19		Company training & Kit inspections	62
"	16.3.19		Voluntary Church Services. Commanding Officers Inspection	62
"	17.3.19		Physical training. Lewis Gun training &c	62
"	18.3.19		Physical training - Cleaning Camp - Afternoon football London Scottish 3 goals 6th South Wales Borderers 2	62
"	19.3.19		Physical training. Coy training &c MAJR R.M ROBERTSON M.C. CAPT J.S MONRO	62
			CAPT W ANDERSON. CAPT C.F BURN. LT II.A WARD LT W COUTTS & CAPT and	
			M.O. I.D STUBBS proceeded to U.K. for demobilization	
	20.3.19		Physical training - Lewis Gun training &c	62
	21.3.19		Physical training. Lewis Gun - Cleaning of Camp &c	62

2/14 London Regiment
LONDON SCOTTISH

Army Form C. 2118.

WAR DIARY
or
INTELLIGENCE SUMMARY

(Erase heading not required.)

Instructions regarding War Diaries and Intelligence
Summaries are contained in F. S. Regs., Part II.
and the Staff Manual respectively. Title pages
will be prepared in manuscript.

Place	Date	Hour	Summary of Events and Information	Remarks and references to Appendices
LE GOUFFRE	22.3.19		Company training and kit inspection	
(LE TOUQUET)	23.3.19		Voluntary Church Service. — Camp inspection.	
	24.3.19		Physical training — Company training etc	
	25.3.19		— do — Cleaning of camp	
	26.3.19		— do — Bathing & cleaning equipment	
	27.3.19		Coy training — Departure of 1/14 GORDON HIGHLDRS proceeded to rejoin their unit.	
	28.3.19		Cleaning Camp — Fatigues etc — ETAPLES Cross country race won by 2/14 Bn LONDON REGT (LONDON SCOTTISH)	
ETAPLES	29.3.19		Battn moved to ETAPLES area during morning — CAPT M R MITCHELL, LT P GEDDES, LT DW BLOW & LT JEDGAR — LT JEDGAR to UK for demobilization	
	30.3.19		Voluntary Church Services — Camp inspection	
	31.3.19		Cleaning Camp etc Lt-Col R.L. OGILBY awarded L'ORDRE DE LA COURONNE and CROIX DE GUERRE	
			Total Bn strength 13 Officers 166 men	

Commdg 2/14 London Regt
London Scottish

SECRET.

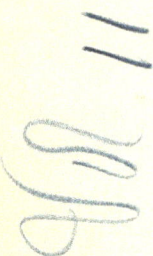

WAR DIARY

OF THE

2/14TH BATTALION LONDON REGIMENT

FOR THE MONTH OF

APRIL 1919

ETAPLES
4/5/19.

CAPTAIN.
COMMANDING 2/14th LONDON REGIMENT.

Army Form C. 2118.

2/14th LONDON REGT
(LONDON SCOTTISH) WAR DIARY
or
INTELLIGENCE SUMMARY.
(Erase heading not required.)

Instructions regarding War Diaries and Intelligence Summaries are contained in F. S. Regs., Part II. and the Staff Manual respectively. Title pages will be prepared in manuscript.

Place	Date	Hour	Summary of Events and Information	Remarks and references to Appendices
E. Gu...	1.12.19		Coy training. Cleaning of camp.	A
(LE TOUQUET)	2.12.19		— do —	A
ETAPLES	3.12.19		— do —	A
	4.12.19		Training. Lewis Gun cleaning & general fatigues. Draft of	A
	5.12.19		15 Officers and 223 men joined Battn from 1/14th London Regt. Battn Coy training. Camp cleaning etc	A
	6.12.19		Church services and Camp inspection by C.O.	A
	7.12.19		Coy training. Lewis Gun cleaning etc	A
	8.12.19		Inspection of Range by Commanding Officer	A
	9.12.19		Route march during morning under Capt L.G Brown M.C	A
	10.12.19		Company training. Physical training. Bathing parades and medical inspection	A
	11.12.19		Coy training. Cleaning Lewis Guns etc	A
	12.12.19		P.T. Coy training and kit inspections	A
	13.12.19		Church services and C.O's inspection of camp	A
	14.12.19		Battn Route March under Capt L.G Brown M.C	A

J. Cameron Capt
Comdg 2/14 Bn London Regt

WAR DIARY / INTELLIGENCE SUMMARY

Army Form C. 2118.

2/1st Bn London Regt (London Scottish)

Place	Date	Hour	Summary of Events and Information	Remarks and references to Appendices
ETAPLES	1.6.19		B Coy proceeded to AUBYN ST VAAST under Capt L D BENNETT M.C. on detached duty.	
	6.6.19		Lieut A Coy Moreton for general fatigues. Lt J McEwan M.C. proceeds Britain from leave to U.K.	
	7.6.19		Coy training. P.T. Lewis gun cleaning etc.	
	8.6.19		Church Services. C.O's inspection of Lewes. Capt L TENNANT M.C. rejoins Bn from leave	
	9.6.19		Coy training. R.S.M. class Lt Col R WHYTE M.C. takes over command of Battn for leave Capt L G BROWN M.C.	
			Church Services. C.O's inspection	
	10.6.19		Divisional Sports at PARIS PLAGE	
	11.6.19		Coy inspections and cleaning of Lewis Guns	
	12.6.19		— do —	
	13.6.19		R.S.M. class	
	14.6.19		Coy training. P.T. etc.	
	15.6.19			
	16.6.19		Lewis Gun cleaning. Football London Scottish 1st Chinese 2?	

M. Stewart Capt
Comd 2/1st London Regt

Army Form C. 2118.

2/4th Bn London Regt
Lothian Battn(?)

WAR DIARY
or
INTELLIGENCE SUMMARY.

(Erase heading not required.)

Instructions regarding War Diaries and Intelligence Summaries are contained in F. S. Regs., Part II. and the Staff Manual respectively. Title pages will be prepared in manuscript.

Place	Date	Hour	Summary of Events and Information	Remarks and references to Appendices
ETAPLES	27.4.19		Church Services. CO's inspection of camp	—
	28.4.19		R.S.M.'s Class. Lewis gun cleaning	—
	29.4.19		— do —	—
	30.4.19		Coy training. R.S.M's Class.	—
			TOTAL BATTN STRENGTH 21 Officers 378 O.R.S.	

J. Brown
Capt
Comd'g 2/4th London Regt.

SECRET.

WAR DIARY

OF THE

2/14TH BATTALION LONDON REGIMENT

FOR THE MONTH OF

MAY 1919

ABBEVILLE.
2-6-1919.

L. Whyte.
LIEUT. COLONEL,
COMMANDING 2/14TH BN. LONDON REGT.
(LONDON SCOTTISH)

1/14th London Regt (London Scottish)

WAR DIARY
or
INTELLIGENCE SUMMARY.
(Erase heading not required.)

Army Form C. 2118.

Place	Date	Hour	Summary of Events and Information	Remarks and references to Appendices
ÉTAPLES	1/5/19		Coy route march under Lt J Allardyce DSO MM. R.S.M's class - guard drills	JH
—	2/5/19		Bathing parade — Coy training etc	JH
—	3/5/19		Medical inspection. Coy training	JH
—	4/5/19		Divine services. C.O's inspection of camp, Lt Col R WHITE MC rejoined from leave	JH
—	5/5/19		Coy training in morning. R.S.M's class in guard drill.	JH
—	6/5/19		— do —	JH
—	7/5/19		— do — B. Coy rejoined	JH
—	8/5/19		Batten from AUBYN ST VAAST.	JH
—	9/5/19		Coy training. Batten took over duties formerly by 7 Royal Scots Regt.	JH
—	9/5/19		Coy training etc	JH
—	10/5/19		Coy training. R.S.M's class, 9 Officers of QUEENS REGT joined Bn for duty	JH
—	11/5/19		Divine services. CO's inspection of camp	JH
—	12/5/19		Coy training. R.S.M's class. Bathing etc	JH
—	13/5/19		— do —	JH
—	14/5/19		Coy training. R.S.M's class. 1 Officer QUEENS REGT joined Bn from duty	JH

Lt Col 1st Bn London Rifles
Comdg 1/14th Bn London Scottish

7/14th Bn London Regt
(London Scottish)

WAR DIARY or INTELLIGENCE SUMMARY

Army Form C. 2118.

Place	Date	Hour	Summary of Events and Information	Remarks and references to Appendices
ETAPLES	15/5/19		Battn ceremonial parade in morning. Divisional service v 7th	
"	16/5/19		Royne Irish Regt regtl 1 – 1. Coy training. Guards, duties etc. RSM's parade.	
"	17/5/19		— do —	
"	18/5/19		Divine services. C.O.'s inspection of camp.	
"	19/5/19		Presentation of colours to Battn by Major Genl G.D. Jeffreys CB CMG DSO. Colour party Lt B.H. Gibson, C.S.M. Williams D.C.M., C.Q.M.S. H.S. rope	
"	20/5/19		P.T. Platoon drill. Specialist training	
"	21/5/19		Inspector Genps. B.T. Musketry training. Squad drill. Manoeuvre Inspection London Scottish v 7th Royne Irish Rifles winners 7th Royne Irish Rifles	
"	22/5/19		Coy cleaning camp during morning etc	
"	23/5/19		— do —	
"	24/5/19		Returning Barrack stores to Q.M. Stores. Divisional Sports at HARDELOT PLAGE	

2/14th London Regt
(London Scottish)

Army Form C. 2118.

WAR DIARY
or
INTELLIGENCE SUMMARY.

(Erase heading not required.)

Instructions regarding War Diaries and Intelligence Summaries are contained in F. S. Regs., Part II. and the Staff Manual respectively. Title pages will be prepared in manuscript.

Place	Date	Hour	Summary of Events and Information	Remarks and references to Appendices
ABBEVILLE	25/5/19		Battn moved to ABBEVILLE and took over duties from 11th E. LANCS Regt.	JM
"	26/5/19		Guards & duties. Settling into camp etc.	JM
"	27/5/19		Guards & duties. R.S.M's class	JM
"	28/5/19		Coy training. Guards. R.S.M's class	JM
"	29/5/19		— do — Cleaning camp etc.	JM
"	30/5/19		— do — — do — R.S.M's class	JM
"	31/5/19		— do — — do — — do —	
			Ration Strength Mr Officers 27 OR 765	

Signed
O.C.
2/14th Bn London Regt
Comdg 2/14th Bn London Regt
(London Scottish)

Army Form W.3091.

Cover for Documents.

S E C R E T.

Nature of Enclosures.

W A R D I A R Y

O F

2/14TH BATTALION. LONDON REGIMENT.
(LONDON SCOTTISH)

FOR MONTH OF JUNE 1919.

Lt-Col.
Commanding 2/14th Battalion London Regiment.
(LONDON SCOTTISH).

Notes, or Letters written.

D.D. 18/6.

HEADQUARTERS,
90TH INFANTRY BRIGADE.

              Herewith WAR DIARY for month of June

1919 please.

ABBEVILLE.
1/7/1919.
                                          Lt-Col.
            Commanding 2/14th Battalion London Regiment.
                     (LONDON SCOTTISH).

2/14 LONDON REGT "LONDON SCOTTISH"

WAR DIARY

INTELLIGENCE SUMMARY

JUNE 1919

Army Form C. 2118.

SECRET

Place	Date	Hour	Summary of Events and Information	Remarks and references to Appendices
ABBEVILLE	1st		Church Parade — Camp Inspection	
	2nd		Coy training — Rgtl's Class — Duties	
	3rd		do — Duties	
	4th		do do	
	5th		Route march — Coy training	
	6th		do	
	7th		Medical Inspn.	
	8th		Baths — Kit Inspection	
	9th		Church Parade — Afternoon Sports (Garrison Athletic)	
	10th		Bn. to ride relay to 880 yds — 1st Ride walk	
	11th		Whit Monday — General Holiday — Duties	
	12th		Coy training — Duties	
	13th		do do	
	14th		do do	
	15th		Route march — Duties	
	16th		Baths Kit Inspection — Duties	
	17th		Church Parade — Camp Inspection	

Army Form C. 2118.

2/14th LONDON REG.T (LONDON SCOTTISH)

WAR DIARY or **INTELLIGENCE SUMMARY**

SECRET

JUNE 1919

(Erase heading not required.)

Place	Date	Hour	Summary of Events and Information	Remarks and references to Appendices
ABBEVILLE	16th		Camp Cleaning — Duties —	
"	17th		do — do —	
"	18th		Coy Training — do —	
"			Bn Swimming Competition (afternoon)	
"	19th		do — do —	
"	20th		do — do —	
"	21st		Baths — Kit Inspection — Duties —	
"	22nd		Church Parade — Camp Inspection — Afternoon: Abbeville Races	
"			Swimming Contest : Bn 1st in Relay, 2nd in Diving.	
"	23rd		Coy Training — Duties —	
"	24th		do — do —	
"	25th		do — do —	
"	26th		do — do —	
"	27th		Baths — Kit Inspection — Duties —	
"	28th		Church Parade — Camp Inspection — Duties.	
"	29th		Coy Training — Duties	

Alytutte
2/14 LONDON R.

S E C R E T.

2/14TH BATTALION LONDON REGIMENT.
(LONDON SCOTTISH)

W A R   D I A R Y.

FOR

MONTH OF JULY 1919.

----------------oOo----------------

2/8/19.

Lieut-Colonel,
Commanding 2/14th Bn. London Regiment.
(LONDON SCOTTISH)

2/14 Bn. London Regiment
(London Scottish)

WAR DIARY
or
INTELLIGENCE SUMMARY. SECRET.

Army Form. C. 2118.

July 1919

Place	Date	Hour	Summary of Events and Information	Remarks and references to Appendices
Abbeville	1st		General holiday. Review and march past of British and French troops in the PORTE DU BOIS ABBEVILLE. Torchlight tattoo in the evening and fireworks display.	
	2nd		Coy Training. Duties	
	3rd		do do	
	4th		do R.C.'s Chard. Duties	
	5th		Baths. Medical Inspection. Kit inspection Duties	
	6th		Church Parades. Camp Inspection Duties	
	7th		Coy. Training. Duties	
	8th		do do	
	9th		Route march. Duties	
	10th		Coy Training do	
	11th		do do	
	12th		Baths. Kit Inspection. Duties. Bn. Road Running Handicap.	
	13th		Church Parades. Camp Inspection	
	14th		French Peace Celebrations. General Holiday. Duties	

Army Form C. 2118.

2/14th Bn. London Regiment (London Scottish) WAR DIARY or INTELLIGENCE SUMMARY. SECRET.

July 1919

Place	Date	Hour	Summary of Events and Information	Remarks and references to Appendices
Abeville	15th.		Coy. Training. Duties	
	16th.		Route march. Duties.	
	17th.		Coy. Training. do	
	18th.		Baths. Kit Inspection. Duties	
	19th.		Peace celebrations. General Holiday.	
	20th.		Church Parade S. Camp Inspection. Duties	
	21st.		Coy. Training. Duties	
	22nd.		do. do	
	23rd.		Route march. R.S.M. class for employed men. Duties	
	24th.		Coy. Training. Duties	
	25th.		do. do	
	26th.		Baths. Kit Inspection. Duties.	
	27th.		Church Parades. Camp Inspection Duties.	
	28th.		Coy. Training. Duties	
	29th.		do. do	
	30th.		Route march. R.S.M's class for employed men. Duties	
	31st.		Coy. Training. Duties	

SECRET

WAR DIARY

of

2/14TH BATTALION LONDON REGIMENT.
(LONDON SCOTTISH).

for

MONTH OF AUGUST 1919.

[signature] Lieutenant-Colonel.
Commanding 2/14th Battalion London Regiment.
(LONDON SCOTTISH).

SECRET

Army Form C. 2118.

WAR DIARY
or
INTELLIGENCE SUMMARY.

2/14th Bn. London Regt.
(London Scottish)
August 1919

(Erase heading not required.)

Instructions regarding War Diaries and Intelligence Summaries are contained in F. S. Regs. Part II. and the Staff Manual respectively. Title pages will be prepared in manuscript.

Place	Date	Hour	Summary of Events and Information	Remarks and references to Appendices
Aberlle	1st		Coy Training. Duties	
	2nd		Batt. Kit Inspection. Medical Inspection Duties	
	3rd		Church Parade - Camp Inspection. Duties	
	4th		Bank Holiday. General Holiday	
	5th		Coy Training. Duties	
	6th		Route March. R.S.M. Cload	
	7th		Coy Training. Duties	
	8th		do do	
	9th		Batto. Kit Inspection. Duties	
	10th		Church Parade. Camp Inspection. Duties	
	11th		Coy Training. Duties	
	12th		do do	
	13th		do Lecture on "Peace Treaty" by Lt. A.Y. Nicholas	
	14th		Route March. R.S.M. Cload. Duties	
	15th		Coy Training. Duties	
	16th		Batto. Kit Inspection. Duties	
	17th		Church Parade. Duties	
	18th		Coy Training. Duties	

SECRET

2/14th Bn. London Regt.
(London Scottish)
August 1919

WAR DIARY
or
INTELLIGENCE SUMMARY
(Erase heading not required.)

Army Form C. 2118.

Page 2.

Place	Date	Hour	Summary of Events and Information	Remarks and references to Appendices
Autville	19th		Coy Training - Duties	
	20th		do	
	21st		Route march - RSMs class Duties	
	22nd		Coy Training. Duties.	
	23rd		Battn kit inspection Duties	
	24th		Church Parade. Camp Inspection Duties	
	25th		Coy Training - Duties	
	26th		do	
	27th		do Duties relieved by 20th Hants. Regt	
	28th		HS men proceeds for dispersal	
	29th		Coy Training	
	30th		Battn kit inspection	
	31st		Church Parade Camp Inspection	

www.ingramcontent.com/pod-product-compliance
Lightning Source LLC
Chambersburg PA
CBHW081444160426
43193CB00013B/2384